'L' ON WHEELS!

A Selection of Humorous Driving Anecdotes

'L' ON WHEELS!

A Selection of Humorous Driving Anecdotes

First Time Publishing

Tel: (0860) 260720

First Time Publishing

First Published 1992

ISBN: 09514415 5 8

Copyright © Brian M. Stratton 1992

Printed in Gt. Britain

Cover Illustration: Ali Clarke

Editor: Brian M. Stratton

☆ ACKNOWLEDGEMENT ☆

Many people have put a great deal of time and effort into making this book possible. Thank you to all of those.

One person who must be singled out, however, is Lynne Lewis, who had the original idea for the book. She also had the tenacity and dogged determination to make sure that it came to fruition. Lynne works as an ADI (approved driving instructor) and is extremely fortunate to have the considerable backing of her family (husband John and daughter Anneliese), who have provided support both practical and spiritual.

Well done Lynne!

The individuals/companies listed below have all helped to bring this book into production.
Their help is gratefully acknowledged.

Bar Code Systems, Kingston
Battle Instant Print, Battle
Blackwell Press, Liphook
Ali Clarke
Dawn Fisher
Pat Howells
Christine Jones
The Sunday Times/Kipper Williams for reproduction of "Pile 'em High"
Mrs. F. Wood

All profits from the sale of this book will go, via Christian Aid, to help the people of
Somalia.

Driving and learning to drive is not always fun, but funny things do happen, and a selection of them has been chosen for this book.

The proceeds will go to Christian Aid for the people of Somalia.

We almost look upon our freedom to learn to drive, to own a car and to travel in it wherever we want to, as basic rights — even in these days of crowded roads and pollution.

There are, however, human rights of far more importance — to food, health care, clean water and shelter for example. We enjoy all of them. The people of Somalia do not.

Many of them are struggling in extraordinarily imaginative and courageous ways to build a happier and healthier future, with more fun and less hardship.

You have helped them by buying this interesting and amusing book.

Thank you.

Michael H. Taylor
Director, Christian Aid.

Other Titles available from First Time Publishing

The Driving Test: Graphic Traffic Version

Hill Start Blues

ADI Part III: Essential Information

ADI Part III and Instructor's Guide

For further information on the above titles
please contact:

First Time Publishing
Tel: (0860) 260720

☆ **Contents** ☆

☆ **Contents** ☆

List of Contributors ☆

in

Alphabetical Order

List of Contributors

☆ ☆

in

Alphabetical Order

Pat Howells

I was, some years ago, after a particularly pleasant luncheon, driving along a quiet road doing very little harm to man or beast when rounding a corner I spied ahead of me a procession. It was the day the circus left town and at the rear of the little convoy, their legs chained together, were four very large jumbos.

Unable to overtake, I pulled in behind the rear elephant's back. Or should it be in the rear of the back elephant's behind? Or even of the behind elephant's rear? Whichever it should have been, I'm sure you get the general picture.

Ahead the traffic lights turned red and we all came gently to a standstill. Now hitherto I had always thought of these particular beasts as being fairly hearty, much given to hauling logs and giving lifts to passing maharajahs. It hadn't occurred to me that sometimes they might be a trifle on the frail side. But thus it proved to be, for whilst I waited for the lights to change, the rear elephant decided to sit down. It was then that the bottom dropped into my world.

I am a little inexperienced when it comes to parking near elephants and I suppose it might be argued that it would have been wiser to have left at least two tails' lengths between the end of the procession and my bumper. With hindsight (literally) I think I would agree, for the great beast sat straight on the bonnet of my car. It was as though a large grey cloud had come across the sun. Presumably the lights turned to "go", for presently the greyness cleared as the elephant lumbered to his feet and disappeared round the corner with the rest of the procession. So intent was I on inspecting the multiple injuries to my limousine that somehow it didn't occur to me to run off in pursuit. I just contented myself with telephoning the police and then got back in the car to await their arrival.

"Nasty mess you've got there, sir," said the sergeant, "what happened?"

"Well, you see, officer, this elephant sat on the bonnet. . . ."

"Would you mind repeating that, sir?"

"Certainly, officer," said I. "About half an hour ago I stopped at these lights and suddenly a great big elephant sat on my bonnet."

"Could I trouble you to step outside the car for a moment, sir?"

I readily complied, whereupon he started to sniff at me in quite the most suspicious way, I do believe I mentioned that I had lunched especially well and it is reasonable to suppose that the aroma of the excellent burgundy lingered round my lips.

"Before you . . . er . . . saw this elephant, sir, had you by any chance consumed any beverage of an intoxicating nature?"

"Well, yes, officer, but I. . . ."

He didn't let me complete the sentence but instead invited me to accompany him to his police station.

Whilst they were busying themselves with their sample (which was negative of course) I asked if I might be allowed to telephone my wife. Permission was granted.

"Hello darling, the most ludicrous thing has happened, I have been arrested."

"Oh no!" she said, in a rather steely way.

"Yes, darling, isn't it silly! My car met with an accident and because I have had a couple of glasses of red wine they won't believe my story. Isn't it absurd?"

"What is your story?" The steel had become positively stainless.

"Well, darling, you see, this elephant sat on my car. Actually there were four of them, but only one . . ."

The phone went dead.

I will never forgive my wife for hanging up on me.

☆ **A Standing Joke 2** — Ted Clements ☆

A driver was clamped on the M25 the other day and it took him four hours to find out that he was actually clamped.

☆ **You and Whose Army? 3** Henry Cooper, OBE, KSG ☆

Christine Jones

I was driving my car accompanied by my former Manager, Jim Wicks (who was at that time about 17 stone) and my twin brother George, when a gentleman on a pushbike pulled out in front of me and, as he did so, I quickly braked, unfortunately he fell off his bike. I pulled over to see that he was not hurt and wound my window down to ask if he was OK. He came over to me and gave me a "right back-hander". With that, Jim Wicks, my brother George and I all got out the car and looked at the gentleman who weighed about eight stone. He looked at me and said, "You think you're brave, just because there's three of you!"

☆ **Pick me up?** — N. Frost ☆

They generally behave themselves, my two mongrel dogs. Very happy to sit in the back of the pick-up while I pop into the post office.

As usual I get into the queue that didn't move at all and seemed to be waiting and waiting.

Suddenly this rather flustered lady rushed in to ask if anyone owned the two dogs who were chasing each other round the shop next door?

Fearing the worst I ran outside — to see the two dogs sitting in the back of a pick-up looking as if butter wouldn't melt!!

Shame they were in the wrong pick-up. . . .

☆ **Look Out!** — A. White ☆

Wilma, who was finding steering a bit difficult, was approaching a give way junction on her third lesson. As she was about to steer to the left her hand caught the windscreen washer control and fired two jets of water up onto the windscreen. Instinctively, she ducked her head down as low as possible, as if to avoid the imagined missiles. She then dissolved into fits of uncontrollable laughter.

Ali Clarke

Shoo! 6 — A. White

Laura, a mild mannered pupil, was driving briskly and smoothly along a dual-carriageway. Suddenly, she took both hands off the steering wheel and started flapping them from side to side. At the same time she was excitedly shouting, "Shoo! shoo! get out the way". All this to a flock of pigeons having lunch in the middle of the road.

Ali Clarke

Martian Law 7 — A. Allan

I remember a pupil called Richard, who, when sitting waiting at traffic lights, used to wait for the red man (incorporated with the lights) to change to green so that he could start to move!

Right Said Fred 8 — A. Allan

Another pupil, called Fred, was driving along at 40mph and kept changing gear unnecessarily. When asked why, he replied, "Oh, I'm just practising!"

Sign of the Times 9 — P. Howie

After his HGV test the candidate was asked by the examiner what kind of signs he might find at the side of a country road. The candidate answered, "Well, signs such as strawberries for sale, pick-your-own, fresh eggs."

The late 1960s and 1970s were the years in which we began to get inter-zoo co-operation really off the ground. Now it is a worldwide movement with the breeding potential of many of our animals in zoos all over the world being pooled and managed as one population, but in those days it was a much more ad hoc affair.

At London, we had two gorillas, the famous Guy and the mate we were able to give him in the later years of his life, Lomie. They got on extremely well with each other, but whether or not their relationship was consummated, it did not result in Lomie becoming pregnant. So, to overcome this setback, we arranged that Lomie should pay a short visit to Bristol Zoo, whose Samson was known to be both willing and able.

Bristol is 115 miles down the M4 from London, about two and a half hours driving time and the tranquillising drugs of the day could guarantee us two hours of sleep, followed by three or four more hours of very tractable drowsiness in Lomie (gorillas are far more placid and benign than they have been cracked up to be. In fact they can be very gentle creatures, though quite capable of using their strength if sufficiently annoyed).

Making sure that we always had two cars in convoy, two vets on hand and two or three other staff as well, we would tranquillise Lomie so that she was fast asleep on a bed at the back of the estate car, with the vet sitting in the back seat keeping watch on her. The ideal was to have her sitting up, though still drowsy, so that she could be walked into the Bristol house when she got there and walked back into her home on return. As it turned out it was the cessation of the car's motion at traffic lights which tended to make her want to sit up and take note of her surroundings.

Christine Jones

Now there are two or three sets of traffic lights between the Motorway and Bristol Zoo and traffic lights are places where drivers and passengers, forced into temporary inactivity, can let their attention wander from the road ahead, to take a look around at the occupants of cars on either side. Many a would-be Romeo, hoping to rest his eyes on the Juliets of his own species established eye-contact with Lomie. What amused me was that almost always there was a look of profound embarrassment on the faces in the neighbouring cars. Obviously they had seen something unusual, but they felt too embarrassed to take a second look and confirm that it really was a gorilla who was giving them a rather sleepy faced glad-eye.

I should add that Lomie had several babies by Samson as a result of these visits.

Director, Chester Zoo (formerly of London Zoo)

☆ **My Brother's Driving Test** — Judy Cook ☆

My brother took his first driving test in North London many years ago. The preliminary part of the test had gone well and the examiner had come to the part involving an emergency stop. The examiner told my brother to drive along until he slammed his clipboard down sharply on his knee — which was the signal for him to do an emergency stop. Nervous, but keen to do well, my brother drove off then stopped dead when the examiner slammed down his clipboard. Then he remembered to look in the rear-view just in time to see a fire-engine going into the back of him.

Needless to say, this incident brought the test to an abrupt halt in more ways than one. The fire-engine was not in fact on the way to an emergency and subsequent examination revealed that it had only very slightly dented the rear of the car my brother was driving. So, after a few caustic comments, the firemen drove off. The examiner returned to the test centre and my brother was left to contact his driving instructor to tell him the test had been aborted and why.

My brother passed his test at the second attempt but admits to still being wary of fire-engines thirty years on.

A Question of Honour — C. Greenaway $\bigstar$ 12

The Japanese gentleman was asked to lead the way out of the waiting room. "YES SIR!!" he replied.

During the drive each time the examiner asked him to do something, the reply was always a respectful and strident "Yes sir".

At the end of the test, the examiner was showing the candidate more signs for him to identify. One of the signs was a blue circle with 30 inside it. The honourable Japanese gentleman thought about it for a moment and said, "30". The examiner, needing more information, asked, "30 what?"

Back came the reply: "30, SIR!"

Pat Howells

$\bigstar$ One Way — A. Lewis $\bigstar$ 13

In common with many religious houses built hundreds of years ago, St. Woolas Cathedral, Newport is circumnavigated by narrow twisty and in this case steep streets. Sensibly, the road has been designated a one way street as there are a couple of blind bends.

Learner drivers (and those who have not the excuse of inexperience) have been known to miss the all important sign and faced with a blind bend and no room to move over to a left lane due to the parked vehicles they tend to almost stop in case oncoming traffic should appear.

Reminding my pupil, Tracy, that the most likely traffic she would encounter might be a skateboarding vicar out of control, she responded by trying to make progress and as we rounded the corner we were met by a large car coming towards us. In shock, we pulled over to a gap in the line of parked cars and as it swept by we just hoped it would make it safely to the end of the one way system!

Some years ago a friend of mine decided to learn to drive. He bought himself a car which I thought rather large and powerful and booked a series of lessons with a large driving school.

He asked me if I would go out with him one evening to give him added experience to which I readily agreed.

All went well this evening until, while turning a corner, he got too close to a cyclist and knocked him off his machine. Nigel immediately stopped and intended to pull into the kerbside to check on the rider, however, he put the gear into reverse by mistake and shot backwards running over the cycle.

The initial damage to the bike was minimal but my friend managed to write it off in his second attempt. Fortunately, the cyclist was uninjured and more concerned about the state of his steed. Nigel promised a new one, which consoled him.

We put the remains of the bike into the boot of the car and took the gentleman home. He lived in a big old house and my friend pulled into the driveway, which I thought a trifle reckless but he managed it without incident. Backing out was a different story, he knocked down half of the outside wall damaging the nearside rear end of his BMW.

All in all it proved a costly lesson and Nigel never lived up to his namesake who achieved fame on the Grand Prix circuit. The only thing they have in common is moustaches!

Until this day Nigel has never developed into a good driver and has the insurance premiums to prove it.

Christine Jones

Friends of ours with a building business sold a house to a young couple who asked if a TVR sports car could be taken as part payment of the deposit. A contract was duly drawn up and a period of time allocated to permit the couple to buy back the car if they wished and could raise the sum of money agreed.

This somewhat unusual arrangement was observed by us over the months and then one day our friends told us on a visit to them that the TVR was now theirs and free of any constraints so would we like a spin in it.

Driving up the village the throaty roar of the sports car attracted quite a few admiring glances and the middle-aged occupants felt the memories of youth seem somehow closer than when they travelled in their usual chariots of family saloons.

Still excited from the drive our friend suggested we each took a trip in his other newly acquired vehicle — the "piglet", a three wheeled tipper truck which had once done service as a Parks and Gardens Department vehicle for a local authority. (The Stella Artois ad on TV shows one in France with a box on the lorry bed.) Fired by a scooter engine reminiscent of those heady mods and rocker days the piglet looked innocent and dull. However, when her full power was unleashed she roared up the hill in the village. People heard her — this they could not deny and hard as they tried to resist eventually they had to look as the noise just kept coming it never seemed to go by, some must have felt they could walk faster!

Yes, the TVR turned a few heads but Piglet turned all of them!

Christine Jones

Pupil to Instructor . . .
"What gear do I go backwards in?"

17 The Lollipop Lady — Anon

Working at a large driving school I was despatched to a new pupil who had failed four times with another driving school. Margaret turned out to be a very mild mannered gentle lady and an absolute delight with the exception of a moment on the first appointment.

Having got Margaret to move away I endeavoured to assess her driving to quicky determine a starting point for instruction and having plenty to think about with problems in all departments — hands, eyes, feet etc. I barely took notice as she told me that the lessons and the little car she had were all bought with "conscience money" because her husband had been having an affair and we weren't to consider the expense at all when planning her tuition.

I made an early decision to take her to a suitable part of the town to practise the manoeuvres and build up a system and co-ordination in her drive and directed her from the busy town. It was mid afternoon.

On the way we came upon the view of a school crossing patrol some distance ahead and as the lollipop lady was walking out to stop traffic I expected Margaret to prepare to stop but instead she went berserk, aiming directly at the figure holding the lollipop, and intent on fulfilling the potential of the vehicle as a lethal weapon accelerated so fiercely at the chosen target the dual braking system was having little effect.

However, the screeching of the engine and squealing of the brakes alerted the children and mothers who parted like the Red Sea and the lollipop and its standard bearer escaped by inches.

Apparently, the lollipop lady was "the other woman"! All lesson appointment times were changed to be sure the school crossing wardens were not on duty and we never went to that area again!

Happily, Margaret discovered her own motivation and passed her test at the next attempt.

18 Thumbs Up — Ted Clements

Sign held up by a hitch-hiker on the approach to the M4 Motorway. "Free brake test — apply here."

An American in London was taking lessons in preparation for the UK test.

Having driven in America, the pupil was much more familiar with automatic cars and was consequently having difficulty with the gears.

Driving along in second gear with the engine screaming, the instructor, wanting to prompt her said, "What gear are you in?"

After a moment's thought, she replied, "A striped top and a black skirt!"

Pat Howells

The learner driver was following a car which was obviously on a touring holiday, and asked if he would get a GB sticker when he passed his test.

"Why do you think you'll get a GB sticker?" enquired the instructor.

"Well, doesn't it mean GETTING BETTER??"

The learner driver replied, "It's all these signs, I'm a slow reader."

Pat Howells

Some friends of ours who are police traffic officers took tremendous interest in the training and examination of our daughter to become an ADI. They were delighted when she passed the Part III exam and curious to hear that not only had she been examined by the Supervising Examiner (ADI) but another SE due to take over part of the area had observed from the back seat of the car.

On patrol one day they came upon an extremely scruffy old Escort and decided that the vehicle needed a closer look. Enquiring as to the ownership of the vehicle they ascertained that the driver had borrowed it that day because his own car had broken down and that the passenger was examining him on the Part II exam. Getting quite excited as he could understand the complexities of these tests having recently lived them second hand our friend asked the examiner if he knew our daughter. On hearing that he was the observer on her recent Part III, a decision was reached. "On your way and good luck, get that tyre changed as soon as possible!"

——— ☆ **Lookie, Lookie, Lookie . . .** — N. Peters ☆ ———

I was out with a pupil who had had many lessons but who would prefer to talk rather than concentrate!

This particular lesson, the objective was the importance of effective observation before emerging.

On approach to a mini-roundabout the directions were . . . "At the roundabout, follow the road ahead, it is the second exit."

We sailed across the roundabout — no one else was around and I was the only one looking anywhere but ahead.

When I asked the pupil why no observation (let alone effective observation) has been taken the reply was . . .

"Oh, at that particular roundabout, you don't have to look to see!"

Some Mothers . . . — L. Lewis **23**

Tommy Freeman was a rather tiresome sort of pupil. He was either still in bed and would need a good shout to rouse him, or not there. When he was not there he would be at the golf club. If he had shoes they would usually be somewhere else. Much of his lesson time would be spent by his instructor on the carpet in front of his father's desk explaining that a cheque was required to proceed and why. Mother would often be at home, usually mowing in wellingtons and a smile and sometimes bikini bottoms too, she never had cash or a cheque.

It was no real surprise, therefore, that scatty Tommy did not pass his test and I insisted that if he rang for more lessons he was, although *extremely* likeable, so much trouble that another instructor should take him.

Another lady instructor accepted the challenge and when she was still unpaid the lesson before the second test she took Tommy to a phone box and told him to phone his father and tell him that since the car was backed up to the kiosk and he couldn't escape, father had better come with cash or a cheque quickly!

Did Tommy ever pass? I don't know, perhaps he's still being held hostage somewhere, barefoot! I do know that when the male instructors heard that his mother liked to garden nude they all volunteered to teach him!

Island Fling — B. Stratton **24**

The driving instructor was on a well deserved holiday, touring Scotland with his wife. Driving down the A832 in north-west Scotland the road ran alongside a loch. Noticing an island out in the distance, the instructor asked his wife "What's that island over there?"

Glancing at the map she replied, "Isle of Ewe".

"Yes, I love you too, but what's the island called?"

Christine Jones

In April 1988 I was to leave this country to work abroad running a Riding School in Corfu, with a Greek friend. This had been a mid life "change of direction" for my husband and myself. (Three years later, after three summers abroad this had to be abandoned, due to the recession at home and not being able to "realise our assets".)

However, I had passed my Driving Test in 1980 when I had been married to my previous husband. I had not sent off my Pass Certificate to have my Provisional Licence updated. Needless to say I never had a Full Driving Licence document. Two years earlier I had had a "narrow escape" when I had been involved in a serious car accident (serious for the cars, that is, not the drivers and passengers, fortunately). My husband's car, which I had been driving was a complete write-off; but the Police were never involved and the Insurance Company paid up, happily.

However, when it came to the time to go to Corfu my husband enquired as to the whereabouts of my Driving Licence. I then had to admit that I had never had a Licence document and subsequently "confessed". After lengthy investigations, DVLC could not come up with the "proof" that I had ever passed my test. I had to take it again. You can guess what happened, I FAILED. I failed after driving thousands of miles each year, for eight years.

I then put in for a second test almost immediately and lo and behold on the day I was confronted with the same, miserable and uncommunicative examiner. I was in an extremely stressed state and as we got ready to begin the test I burst into floods of tears and "confessed". I told him I was emigrating (well it was nearly true); and that I had been driving for years and that I couldn't bear if if he failed me: since I had surely proved I was competent. (I didn't mention the accident in which my husband's beuatiful POLO car had been written off.) The test proceeded in strained silence and I think because he could not bear any more feminine hysterical outbuursts (he seemed a reserved person) he reluctantly told me I had passed. (Two out of three — well that's what I always maintain … not bad, really!)

What Emergency? **26** — B. Stratton

Christine Jones

Mrs. Bracewell absent-mindedly fingered her pearls as the examiner droned on at her. What did this silly man want her to do? Something about an emergency stop . . . they set off, the examiner heading for a quiet road to carry out the exercise.

Distracted by seeing a friend (dressed in beige, for goodness sake!), Mrs. Bracewell was only vaguely aware of the examiner slapping the windscreen with his notebook.

After another 15 seconds or so had passed, the examiner again slapped the windscreen. Mrs. Bracewell was by now becoming irritated by the silly little man and his annoying ways. Although she knew she wasn't supposed to talk to the examiner she would have to say something.

For a third time, the examiner slapped the windscreen.

In a voice heavy with sarcasm Mrs. Bracewell turned to the examiner and asked, "Haven't you got that fly, yet?"

You Type of People **27** — D. Clarke

Shortly after the parallel park exercise was introduced as part of the driving test, a learner driver was practising the manoeuvre in a quiet suburban street in well heeled Bromley.

After watching the proceedings for a few minutes from behind the net curtains, one of the householders came out and approached the tuition vehicle. She tapped on the instructor's window and when he opened it she said in a superior voice, "I say, we're not going to get a lot of you type of people down here doing this are we?"

Ali Clarke

Christine Jones

☆ **It's a Dog's Life** — Little & Large ☆

28

This businessman friend of ours drove into London's East End in his brand new "K" reg (well it would be but he had a set of personalised number plates) top of the range German executive saloon.

He was a bit concerned to find that the street where he had an appointment was in a rather dodgy area.

As he got out of the car some kids approached him and asked, "Can we mind your car mate?"

"No it's alright," he replied, indicating Max his rottweiler lurking in the back.

Returning to the car an hour later he noticed that all four tyres were flat. There was also a scruffy piece of paper tucked under the windscreen wiper. Opening it up he read . . .

"Get your dog to blow them up for you!"

☆ **Original Chippendale** — Ted Clements ☆

29

The IAM's Chief Examiner was once described by a journalist as: "A unique part of Chiswick High Road furniture." He did not say if it was modern or antique. I suspect the latter because another journalist asked what he did in the police force and the answer was: "The technical adviser to Dixon of Dock Green." My word that dates him!

Having failed her first driving test in London, where we were then living and working, my wife decided to apply for the re-test in our home town of Monmouth in an attempt to avoid the long wait which would be inevitable if she re-booked the test in London. "We'll make it a surprise visit to the family," she said, "We have been working hard lately and it is time we had a break from work and London. We'll go down the night before, stop in a hotel and then I can drive up to the front door and honk the horn and wave my licence when I have passed."

She drove all the way down from London very well indeed and I was beginning to feel confident and relaxed about it all. We checked into the hotel in good time and decided to go out for a drink before dinner. We had hardly decided to do so when the heavens opened and torrential rain set in. The plan was quicky amended and I was nominated to drive to a suitable country pub, where I could have a soft drink whilst my wife enjoyed a sherry — the theory being that I could catch up later when the car was safely parked in the hotel car park.

It was still raining heavily when we reached the pub, so I dropped my wife off at the foot of the steps leading up to the front door, so that she could make a dash for the entrance whilst I parked the car. When I ran back from the car park she was calling out from the pub door, "We are too early they are not open yet." "Back to the car then," I yelled. Before she had time to reply she disappeared from sight below a low parapet wall, I raced up and found her flat on her back and obviously in pain.

On return to the hotel it was obvious that the injury was serious so I drove to the nearest Casualty Department, some 20 miles away. The doctors could not be sure as to the diagnosis and it was eventually agreed to inject my wife with a massive dose of powerful pain killer and admit her overnight. Having seen her to the Ward I returned to the hotel where eventually I got to bed at about 3 a.m. I tossed and turned for a few hours, and then gave up all hope of sleep, settled the bill and went back to the hospital.

I was shocked at my wife's appearance, she is normally of a stoical disposition but I found her ashen faced, tearful and obviously in great pain. Her question however was, "How about my driving test?" "No chance, love," I replied.

The injury was eventually diagnosed as a severe posterior dislocation of the shoulder, which was treated and after a further night in hospital I drove my long suffering wife back to London, still without the coveted "Pink slip".

My wife however, is nothing if not determined and she immediately booked a re-test in Monmouth. As the appointed date approached it became clear that I would not be able to accompany her for business reasons so she opted to travel by train, visit the family, and retain a local driving school to give her a few lessons and take her for the test. She promised to phone me as soon as she had taken the test whatever the outcome. At the appointed time the phone rang on my desk and from the tone of my wife's voice I knew all was not well. Attack being the best form of defence I said, "O love you haven't failed I hope." "No" came the reply, "I have neither passed nor failed." She then went on to explain that she was having a final run out with the instructor about half an hour before the test when the car broke down, in her words, "Bits actually fell off the engine." Another lost test.

When she got home we came to the conclusion that once could be an accident and twice could be a coincidence, but a third attempt might be visited with a disaster, so she reluctantly re-joined the long queue at our local north London test centre. A decision which, if taken earlier, could have saved a good deal of pain and suffering and a not inconsiderable sum of money. That's motoring though.

☆ **Dead Slow 31 — T. Wright** ☆

The driving test was almost over, just four or five minutes to go. Rounding a bend they came upon a funeral procession. The learner driver tagged on at the end and drove along at 20 m.p.h. and despite several opportunities, didn't overtake. The examiner, somewhat exasperated by this, turned to the learner and said, "Madam, did you know the deceased?"

Christine Jones

Christine Jones

☆ It's For You **32** — A. Jay ☆

Driving past an open phone box, the phone started ringing. The learner driver was concentrating heavily on her driving and was only vaguely aware of a phone ringing.

"Is that your car phone?" she asked.

"No there isn't a phone in the car," replied the instructor.

"Oh," said the learner, "I thought you all had those cellulite phones?"

"On the money I earn — fat chance of that," said the instructor.

☆ Cool Customer **33** — B. Stratton ☆

Sitting in a queue of slow moving traffic at roadworks, the learner driver was getting more and more annoyed at drivers coming up the outside lane and cutting in just before the cones.

As yet another driver came alongside preparing to cut in, the learner looked over at him and said, "Look at him, cool as a queue-jumper!!"

Christine Jones

☆ Broken Down **34** — Anon ☆

Stranded on the hard shoulder of the motorway the driver called in the A.A. After a brief inspection, during which it became clear that the car wasn't going to move under its own steam. . . .

"Well mate," said the patrolman, "it's going to be a duchess."

"A what?" said the motorist.

"A Tow Job."

Fare Comment — D. Kelly **35**

A friend of mine and her six-year-old daughter were in a mini cab travelling to visit relatives. The route took them along a certain road in south London frequented by working girls.

"What are all those ladies waiting for?" asked Emma.

Not wanting to get involved in a discussion her mum answered, "They are waiting for their husbands."

Hearing this the minicab driver said, "Why don't you tell her the truth — they're prostitutes!"

At this the little girl asked her mother, "Mummy, do these prostitutes have children?"

"Yes dear, they're called mini cab drivers!!"

A Right Two and Eight — B. Stratton **36**

Hither Green sounds like an idyllic country retreat set in rolling pastures — rural life personified.

In actual fact it is a work-a-day suburb of South-East London; and home to a test centre. One day, three of us instructors were waiting outside for the tests to finish. The examiner got out of my pupil's car and made his way over to me.

"You didn't tell me I'd need an interpreter for that one!" he said, nodding over to my car.

"What do you mean?" I asked, puzzled.

"Well I showed her a sign for the countdown markers on the motorway and asked her to identify it. She looked at it and said, 'Oh yeah, that's the thingibobs on the wotsisname'."

37 ☆ **Test of Faith** — L. Clark ☆

It was the end of the driving test. The examiner said to the Clergyman, "I'm sorry that you haven't passed. . . ."

Disheartened, the Clergyman looked out of the window, raised his eyes heavenwards and said, "You weren't much help to me this morning were you??"

Christine Jones

38 ☆ **The Thumbs' Crew** — M. Bowman ☆

I know a lady driver who is always in a hurry and really does not like letting any other drivers pull out in front of her . . . except bus drivers that is.

Why?

Because she loves it when they put their hands out of the window and give the "thumbs up".

39 ☆ **The Rain in Spain** — G. Peacock ☆

The learner driver was getting on very well with her lessons. Despite her Spanish upbringing she was coping well with the language and the confusing conditions.

One rainy day, getting in the car at the start of her lesson she said to the instructor, "I have never seen so much rain, look at all those puddles."

With her charming accent she had pronounced this "poodles".

The instructor turned to her and said, "Yes, it's been raining cats and dogs."

Ali Clarke

☆ Feet First — M. Quinn ☆ 40

Christine Jones

Trying to park in St. Tropez is never easy. Even less so at night, after a tiring drive with a car packed full of luggage and kids.

Turning into a congested side street I was delighted to see a gap in a row of parked cars.

As I was reversing into the space, a passing Frenchman stopped to watch.

"How much space behind?" I asked him.

"A meter," came the reply.

More than I thought — just over three feet. I continued reversing at a slow but steady speed. CRUNCH!!!

The Frenchman was shrugging and looking at the back of the car, crunched against a parking meter.

"I told you — there was a meter behind you!!"

☆ Bird Brains — D. Murray ☆ 41

One afternoon on top of a hill in Ridgeway Lynne, my instructor, informed me that today's lesson was the use of arm signals to show other drivers what course of action you intend to take. Just in front of our car where we were parked was another car with office staff eating their lunch. We rolled down our windows and Lynne asked me what course of action I would take to let other road users know I intended to slow down, so I put my arm straight out of the window and flapped it up and down. All of a sudden, Lynne decided also to put her arm out of the window and pretend we were a bird just about to take off. After the initial embarrassment I looked up to find all the office staff looking at us laughing hysterically!

My Friend Darren — D. Murray

My friend Darren was driving along a road in Pontypool with his music very loud, when all of a sudden all the cars that were in front of him started to move out of the way. Not looking in his mirrors Darren decided to overtake them all. Suddenly he decided to look in his mirror and found a fire engine very close to his bumper with the siren full blast and all the blue lights flashing and all the firemen leaning out of their windows shouting at him. Very quickly he pulled in and had some dirty looks as they drove by.

☆ All Change — N. Frost ☆

"What gear could you have been in by now?"

Christine Jones

"I don't know — how many are there?"

Brass Monkeys — Ted Clements ☆

After a spate of indecent exposures in quiet Dunblane recently, a top traffic policeman told the reporter: "I am not too concerned — they tend to drop off in the winter."

Christine Jones

☆ Mr. Stevens? — C. Butler ☆

At the grand old age of 82, my most senior pupil had, at the seventh attempt, finally passed his test.

As he got out of the car I said to him, "Congratulations, let me shake you by the hand."

Offering me his hand he said, "At my age you just hold it — it shakes by itself!"

☆ Far Too Much — J. Russell ☆

I'd promised to take some details about the driving school to a new pupil. After parking outside I walked up the path to the front door. On the doorstep was a large rough coated mongrel dog who looked as though he belonged to the house.

I rang the door bell and was invited in. As I walked into the hall the dog followed me in and as I sat down it lay down on the floor — obviously at home.

As I discussed the structure of the driving lessons, price and other details, the dog was breaking wind in a noisy and very smelly manner.

The family acted as if nothing was wrong so I too, ignored it and assumed their dog was always "relaxing" in this way.

Eventually though I couldn't stand much more of it and made my excuses to leave.

As I was walking down their path one of the family called out after me, "Oi, aren't you going to take your dog with you??"

☆ Follow the Dotted Lines . . . — J. Banks ☆

Instructor to pupil: "Why are these long white lines down the middle of the road?"

Pupil: "So they know where to put the cat's eyes!"

It was our Silver wedding anniversary and we decided to celebrate in style by touring in California and visiting an old FBI chum, with whom I had worked, and who had been posted to the Golden State.

My chum Bill met us as arranged at Los Angeles airport but instead of leading me to hire-car, which he had promised to arrange, he drove us to his lakeside home in his own vehicle. "What about our hire car?" I asked. "Don't worry," he replied, "You will be staying with us tonight and I'll take you to pick up your car tomorrow, I have managed to arrange a good discount."

Next morning he took me to an impressive car showroom where the man in charge showed me what looked like a low flying aircraft, "Do you like it sir?" he enquired. "I can let you have it for . . .," quoting a price that I could hardly believe, "Plus tax and insurance of course." I hastened to sign the rental agreement, and after the briefest of explanations of the controls edged out on Ventura freeway. There seemed to be more dials, switches and controls in that car than on the average aircraft, but I eventually made it back to the house where my wife was waiting to set off on our tour.

We set off for the Pacific Coast highway via the spectacular Malibou Canion Road, but we had hardly got into the canyon when my wife closed her window to exclude the smog smell which made the air redolent with the tang of rotting eggs. Shortly afterwards she closed her eyes saying that the hairpin bends were giving her vertigo and I thought to myself, "God we travel half way around the world for my wife to ride through the scenery with her eyes closed and the window shut!"

Anybody who has been married for a quarter of a century can probably visualise the atmosphere that had built up between my wife and I, the scene resembled an old silent movie, all facial expressions and no dialogue.

As we progressed towards Malibou beach I remembered from a previous visit, the excellent seafood restaurant built out on stilts over the sea, and I resolved to repair the damage by taking my wife there for an early lunch. I turned off the highway into the enormous car park, and leaving my wife in the car strode across to check on the availability of tables. Having been successful in getting a table I walked back to the car and catching my wife's eye, gave her the thumbs up. As I neared the hired car I could see her fiddling with the door, "What's up?" I enquired, and she told me that on leaving the car the door had stuck in the locked mode but in a half-open position. No amount of fiddling with the key and the central locking button would free the door so I asked my wife what exactly she had done to get in such a fix. Before I could stop her she went around to the drivers door and said, "I only did this," and promptly got the driver's door stuck and locked in the same way.

So there we were with a rented car in an unusable condition about 30 miles away from the nearest friendly faces, not really the ideal start to a motoring holiday. The car park was guarded by an enormous man, bronzed and wearing a police type uniform complete with holstered pistol on hip. I approached this formidable figure, who on hearing of my plight gave me that look that the Americans have given to the British for years and reaching back into his sentry box, produced an enormous crowbar-like implement.

Without a word he bore down on my car, exerted his considerable strength to lever the door locks open, and yet never damaged the locking mechanism or put a scratch on the paintwork. He grandly waved away my offered tip with the ubiquitous, "Have a nice day" as he again took up his post at the car park entrance.

The subsequent lunch was a complete success and despite a sticky start the California tour turned out to be even more enjoyable than we had expected, in fact I got so attached to that car that I was quite reluctant to return it to the hire firm before heading for the airport and home.

☆ **A Fishy Story** — Leslie Thomas ☆

The day I passed my driving test was the same day that my daughter was born — 36 years ago. So delighted was I at getting my full licence (at the first attempt!) that I told the driving examiner that had my new daughter been a son, I would have called the baby after him.

"I would not have advised that," he said. "My Christian name is Halibut!"

It was a sticky hot Summer day in London and I had been working on files at my desk all the morning. Contrary to the popular TV image senior police officers spend far more time wrestling with paperwork than they do arresting villains. I readily accepted the necessity for paperwork but it was never the most enjoyable aspect of my work.

I decided to skip lunch in the senior officers dining room in favour of a stroll in Regents Park. I bought some fresh fruit from a shop in Albany Street and set off through Chester Terrace Mews for the Park.

As I ambled along the tree lined avenue towards the bandstand I idly watched a lady unsuccessfully trying to reverse a large Mercedes car bearing diplomatic plates, into a gap barely large enough to receive it. When I was level with the vehicle a stunningly beautiful Asian lady got out of the car and said to me, "Excuse me sir, do you drive?" When I replied in the affirmative she asked me to park her car for her. Not wishing to appear ungallant, and being a Hendon trained police driver I got into the driving seat to oblige. I drove out into the carriageway to get a better angle to reverse into the gap, and was astonished when I glanced over my shoulder to see a delightful gurgling, almond eyed infant strapped into a safety seat in the back.

Having parked the car I returned the keys to the owner, produced my Warrant card and began to deliver a lecture on the foolhardiness of allowing a total stranger into such a wonderful car, particularly as it contained a baby. Before I could develop my theme, she raised an elegant hand fluttered her eyes and said, "There was no risk with you sir, you have such a trusting face."

I was floored but could manage nothing better by way of reply than, "Madam there simply is no answer to that so I will bid you good afternoon."

──────── ☆ **Seen it all Before 51** — Ted Clements ☆ ────────

A lady candidate taking her IAM test and giving a driving commentary
simply said: "Man in front flashing — will not interfere with me."

Ali Clarke

☆ Ask a Silly Question **52** — D. Clarke ☆

Driving down a narrow road with parked cars on each side, the learner driver was getting very close to the stationary vehicles.

The trainee instructor turned to the pupil and asked, "Don't you know how close you are going to these parked cars?" . . . to which the learner driver scornfully replied, "No, I'm not sitting that side of the car."

☆ Malcolm X **53** — Anon ☆

As happens at most driving test centres, when the pupils have departed, the instructors often sit around and discuss life, the universe and everything.

Malcolm, an unpopular instructor — all mouth and opinions, — was whingeing about . . . well about everything really, when he added: ". . . and what's more, all of my pupils seem to take an instant dislike to me. I can't understand it!"

Another instructor summed up everyone's thoughts when he said, "Well, Malcolm, it saves time!"

☆ Losing Faith **54** — Ted Clements ☆

A very young traffic policeman stopped a car for speeding. He then discovered that he was a man of the cloth. The PC apologised but the vicar put him at ease and said: "You have your job to do" and invited the young policeman round for tea on Sunday. The policeman thanked him and as the vicar drove away he called out: "Bring your mother and father and I will marry them!"

Noisy Neighbours — N. Frost 55

He had had a terrible day at the office and to cheer himself up was playing a favourite tape as he drove home.

You know how it is, the music gets turned up at the best bits and never seems to get turned down again.

Coming up to red traffic lights he pulled up next to another car without much thought. However he was brought back to reality with the sound of a horn being blasted at him — looking round at the car next to him to see what the problem was he saw the driver gesticulating frantically.

Turning down the music to hear what the problem was, he heard quite clearly the driver next door yelling — "Would you turn the **!! music down, I'm on the phone!!

Seeing Double? — D. Sheedy 56

Working for a large driving school and having the distinctive logo all over the car has its advantages . . . and its disadvantages.

On the way to collect a new pupil I drove onto a busy estate and followed the instructions exactly, to find after five minutes I was back where I started from.

Not being known for my navigation skills I decided it was obviously driver error so I tried again. No luck! It can't be that far I thought and set off once more. Back where I started from.

Help was at hand when I spotted a postman coming down the road — when I stopped him to ask directions to the house he looked very confused. He explained that I was in fact very near the house but was I sure of the address — he'd already seen one of our driving school cars going out that way about ten minutes ago!

No Right Turn — J. Laing   ☆

Barry, a mate of mine, was driving his wagon through a town in Norfolk when he came up behind an ancient Austin A35 being driven by an elderly gent wearing hat and driving gloves.

Being an old car, the signals were of the trafficator sort, which stick out from the side of the car.

The right trafficator was out, and so Barry expected him to turn off shortly. Not so!! Several right turns came and went but the old gent just carried on, straight ahead. Eventually red traffic lights brought the A35 (still with trafficator indicating right) and Barry to a stop.

Right, thought Barry, I'll just have a quick word. Seeing Barry approaching the old gent wound down the window and said, "What is it?" in a tone reserved for servants and brush salesmen.

"Well sir," said Barry in most "umble" tones — "I was just wondering if you were going to be turning right at some stage?"

"Certainly not, I'm going straight ahead."

"In that case," said Barry, "you won't be needing this" and snapped off the offending trafficator and threw it in to the car to land on the old gent's lap.

Light Work — J. Laing   ☆

A few years ago I was driving my H.G.V. and trailer through Shropshire. At some roadworks there were temporary traffic lights. As I came to a stop I realised that there wasn't sufficient room for my wagon to get through. No problem, I thought, I'll just move the temporary lights to one side. As I picked up the traffic light the three supporting feet fell off the bottom of the pole. Try as I might I could not get the feet back on the pole. As I put one on another fell off and so on! By this time the lights had gone through several changes and being really cheesed off by now, I eventually left the lights propped up against a pile of gravel. At least I got my lorry through!

A Bit of a Squeeze — J. Riddle — 59

(Ladies only please)

You know the feeling when you are just a tiny bit overweight and you try to get into the best dress — and the zip won't move. Imagine the trauma of the poor woman who phoned her neighbour in a panic. She couldn't get into the present her husband had just bought her . . . a beautiful new sports car!!

Hill Start Blues — J. Bracewell — 60

One of my pupils wanted to take the test in her own car. Despite trying to dissuade her, she duly went up for her test in the family car with her mum "riding shotgun".

Unfortunately the car had an "iffy" handbrake and the examiner had to help her on several hill starts. The candidate was getting more and more flustered by this. In the town centre, a busy junction on a hill proved to be the final straw.

Feeling unable to cope, she suddenly switched off the engine, opened the car door and ran off! Somewhat bemused, the examiner made sure the car was safe and walked back to the test centre to explain the situation to the candidate's mother.

There is a happy postscript to this story. She took a second test (in a school car) and passed without incident.

Ali Clarke

☆ **Right Confused** — Anon ☆ —————

Met a couple of old dears who went right around a very busy roundabout, then proceeded to go the right-hand side of a "keep left" bollard and drive down the right-hand side of double white lines — the fast lane of the on-coming traffic. A multiple pile-up was avoided thank goodness, and they were finally forced over into the correct lane by the on-coming traffic!

This example by the way, endorses my view that 70 year olds onwards should re-take driving tests!!

————— ☆ **Golders Green Blues** — Ted Clements ☆ —————

A motorist driving through North London came across an accident and the little Jewish driver was lying in the road and the motorist asked: "Are you comfortable," and he said: "I make a living."

————— ☆ **There's None So Blind** — M. English ☆ —————

An Instructor was so impressed with a new blind spot mirror that he was concentrating on it and moved off and collided with a car not in blind spot!

————— ☆ **Shiny Happy People** — A. White ☆ —————

A lady driver was stopped by the police for speeding.

The officer said to her, "Madam, didn't you realise you were exceeding the speed limit?"

"Well, officer," she says, "I've only just cleaned and polished the car and because it's so shiny and slippery it's going faster than it used to!"

"Mind that Pike!" — L. Lewis

Bob was enjoying his second day as a newly qualified driving instructor. The elderly lady he was teaching was responding to his instruction and he felt quite relaxed in his work.

Taking her out along the moors between Newport and Cardiff she was improving her steering on the flat windy roads with the lovely open views.

However, the moment was short lived as it became apparent she was failing to take a right hand bend and Bob, anxious to show his dual steering skills moved his hand to guide the steering wheel and thus keep the car on course.

The elderly lady unfortunately mistook this gesture for an assault and leaving hold of the steering wheel rained blows on Bob with both hands who had to defend himself. With no-one at the wheel what else could the car do but roll off the road into the reen (dyke) which it fitted exactly.

The only way out was through a window, but not until the car had filled with water.

All that was visible of the car from the bank was the roof sign.

Both instructor and pupil survived and the lady even drove the "rescue car" away from the scene, leaving a very wet patch behind.

Send for the Cavalry — C. Pointer

It's always difficult to find a parking space in the City Centre and being late for an important appointment I was tempted into parking on a "residents only" bay.

I thought I'd try some charm on the traffic warden who would not miss my illegally parked car . . . I left a note to say . . .

"Broken down — gone to fetch the cavalry."

However, it didn't work because when I got back to the car I had a parking ticket and a note from the traffic warden which said . . .

"The cavalry are too late — the Indians have already been!!"

Trigger Happy — M. English

An Instructor reminded his learner to look round because you never know what's behind. The learner was startled to find a large horse looking through the car window.

Write and Wrong — Ted Clements

After receiving a very rude letter from an annoyed motorist The Chief Examiner of the IAM replied: "I hope you don't drive like you write letters."

Snap? — G. Keeble

A classic car they called it. Not that we treated it in any special way; I drove it to and from work each day. I suppose you could call it a working classic. There were very few of them about and each time we saw another one it brought out a sense of camaraderie — thumbs up, lights flashing, etc.

Eventually though, circumstances forced us to sell the old girl and buy something more mundane and practical.

A week after selling the classic, I was waiting at red traffic lights, mind idly wandering, when a car pulled up alongside. I immediately recognised it as a sister of my old car. I was thrilled to see another one. Catching the driver's eye I gestured to my own car and gave the thumbs up, smiled and gave the impression of great-cars-aren't-they,-don't-build-'em-like-this-any-more, etc., etc.

The driver and occupants of the other car were looking at me rather strangely, giving forced half-smiles and glancing at each other and then over to me with obvious bemusement. I couldn't understand why.

As we drove away from the lights the penny dropped. I suddenly remembered; I wasn't driving my old classic any more. . . .

☆ A Papal Moss — Anon ☆

The Pope was on a visit to England and was travelling from London to Birmingham. Worried that he was going to be late, the Pope urged the driver to go faster. The driver, however, was worried about losing his licence and refused to do more than 70 mph.

Frustrated by this, the Pope ordered him to pull up at the next service station. They swapped seats and the Pope roared off down the motorway and was soon cruising along at 120 mph.

The inevitable happened. They got stopped for speeding. The traffic policeman looked at the driver and then at the rear seat passenger. Not wanting to cause a diplomatic incident he radioed in for advice.

"I've just stopped someone important — very important."

Control replied, "Well who is it?"

"I'm not sure."

"Well is it John Major?"

"No, more important than him."

"Michael Heseltine?"

"No, but it must be someone *really* important — he's got the Pope driving him!"

☆ Driving on the Other Side — Ted Clements ☆

A very keen and supportive IAM member for a number of years left in his will strict instructions to have his IAM badge suitably fixed to his tombstone.

☆ Water on the Brain — L. Lewis ☆

A lady driver phoned her husband at work to tell him that the car had water in the carburettor. He graciously said, "Don't worry, dear, where is the car? I'll get a mechanic to come out."

"Unfortunately," she replied, "it's in the river."

They All Look the Same to me — M. Khan

The subject of motorbikes came up at the test centre the other day. One of the instructors remembered the case of an examiner conducting a motorbike test a few years ago.

In those days the examiners watched the candidates ride around and got them to perform various exercises. On this particular occasion, after a few minutes of general riding, the examiner motioned the pupil to pull up beside him. The examiner then explained that he wanted him to ride round certain roads — a sort of circuit — and at some point he would jump out and shout "stop!" The candidate would then be required to perform an emergency stop.

The motorcyclist rode off and went round the route as described. As he turned the final corner he saw the examiner lying flat on his back in the road with three or four people gathered around. Another motorcyclist, his machine lying in the road, was explaining to one of the bystanders, ". . . I was just riding along minding my own business when all of a sudden, this nutter jumped out in front of me!!"

Body Work — M. English

An Instructor fed up with teaching put an ad in the local paper looking for a driving job. He got a phone call in the middle of the night and was asked if he'd like to move a body for £500. He didn't take up the offer.

Free Wheeling — F. Wood

Broken down on the motorway, the driver returned from making his emergency call to find his truck jacked up and a man removing the wheels.

"What the hell are you doing?" the driver demanded.
Without looking up, the man replied, "Don't worry, I only want a couple, you can have the rest."

─────── ☆ **Missing Link** – F. Wood ☆ ───────

Stopped for having no number plate on his trailer the driver protested, "It was there this morning."

The sceptical police officer smirked, "Well, it isn't there now."

"In that case," said the driver, "I want to report a theft."

─────── ☆ **Playing to the Crowd** – B. Stratton ☆ ───────

It was a Saturday afternoon lesson with Matthew, who was quite a good pupil. I'd planned to get him to do an emergency stop in the road that runs alongside the football stadium. I wanted to arrive there at 3.30 p.m. — by that time everyone should be inside the ground.

I gave the signal to "STOP!", and Matthew brought the car to a prompt and controlled halt. Just at that precise moment there came a roar, followed by applause, from the stadium. Obviously a goal had just been scored.

Matthew, not realising what the noise was, looked at me quizzically. I said, "They obviously liked your emergency stop as well!!"

─────── ☆ **Sarah's Boob** – L. Lewis ☆ ───────

Inviting Sarah, who was 7½ months pregnant, to identify the sign for uneven road surface she told me it warned of a double hump back bridge. Encouragingly, I asked her to try again and when she was stumped I asked her what she had got beginning with B which not everybody had, looking for bump as an answer. "Boobs" came the reply without any hesitation!

79

June, a prison visitor, had finished her talk to the inmates and was walking out to the car park when it gradually dawned on her that she couldn't find her car keys. Looking inside her locked car she saw them, in the ignition. Damn. Swallowing her pride she went back to the Governor's office and explained the situation.

"Wait a moment," said the Governor, "I'll find one of the lads who's in for nicking cars!"

He returned a few minutes later with a prisoner who claimed he could "get into any car within five seconds".

June was secretly impressed by this and thought "this should be worth seeing!"

The three of them trooped out to the car park. The prisoner looked at June's car and said, "No problem. Watch this," and promptly picked up a brick and threw it through the side window!

80

His lorry had broken down again. The driver was going to phone Head Office and tell them exactly what he thought of them and their clapped out wagons. Unfortunately for him, the phone was answered by the managing director.

After listening to the driver's abusive tirade the managing director said, "Do you know who you're speaking to?"

During the stunned silence that followed, it gradually dawned on the driver who he was speaking to. Thinking quickly, he replied, "Yes, I do and do you know who you're talking to?"

"No."

"Well," said the driver, "that's alright then," and put the phone down.

Splash Course — see story opposite

── ☆ **Splash Course!** 81 — C. Greenaway ☆ ──

Driving instructor Clive Greenaway found he had been well and truly dropped in it when vandals threw the sign off the top of his car into the river in Poole.

Former tank instructor Clive arrived to find a crowd of people peering down at the water.

"They thought the whole car had gone in leaving just the sign sticking out of the water — fortunately it was just the sign which had gone in and we managed to fish it out!"

Clive, whose Impact School of Motoring specialises in week-long crash courses, recently suffered a crash course of his own — when another car smashed into him at traffic lights, with considerable Impact.

Crunch . . . the driving school certainly lived up to its name when learner Damian Parmenter signed up for lessons.

Damian, aged 27, a Ministry of Defence office worker, only got to his sixth lesson with the Impact School of Motoring when . . . smash . . . a car crashed into the back of his J-reg Fiesta (above) as he was waiting at traffic lights.

"We all had a good laugh about it — I soon found out what they meant by a crash course," he recalled.

But Damian, of Broughton Avenue, Bournemouth, who was attracted by the 666 in the school's telephone number, seems to be having the devil's own job getting through his test — he took it on Monday and failed.

── ☆ **In Your Own Time** — J. Laing ☆ ──

Arriving at a busy junction, the learner driver was confused by the multiplicity of traffic signs.

After missing several opportunities to emerge, the instructor said to the learner, "What are you waiting for?"

"It's all these signs," replied the learner, "I'm a slow reader."

── ☆ **Upside Down** — J. Banks ☆ ──

Instructor to pupil: "Why is the give way sign upside down?"
Pupil: "So the words fit in easier!"

── ☆ **The Fog Code?** — J. Laing ☆ ──

It was a very foggy night. The old man was peering over the steering wheel and driving along at a steady speed. All of a sudden there was a loud bang as he drove into the vehicle in front.

Both drivers got out and the driver whose vehicle had been hit said, "Why don't you look where you're going?" to which the old man replied indignantly, "And why don't YOU go where you're looking!"

"Do they read the Highway Toad?"

"Two Wheels on my Wagon . . ."

"Well, orderz is orderz . . ."

"Is it coming or going?"

SOME FAMOUS LAST WORDS

"But I had right of way"

"I know *every* inch of this road"

"It's OK, the lights have only *just* turned to red"

"Which is the brake?"

"What stop sign?"

"If you brake carefully, worn tyres don't matter a bit"

"I drive down this road *every* day — there's never anything coming"